Animals in My Yard

Deer

by Amy McDonald

BELLWETHER MEDIA
MINNEAPOLIS, MN

Blastoff! Beginners are developed by literacy experts and educators to meet the needs of early readers. These engaging informational texts support young children as they begin reading about their world. Through simple language and high frequency words paired with crisp, colorful photos, Blastoff! Beginners launch young readers into the universe of independent reading.

Blastoff! Universe

Reading Level — Grade K

Grades 1-3

Grade 4

Sight Words in This Book 🔍

a	for	in	see	you
and	from	is	the	
big	have	it	them	
brown	he	look	they	
can	her	people	this	
eat	his	run	with	

This edition first published in 2021 by Bellwether Media, Inc.

No part of this publication may be reproduced in whole or in part without written permission of the publisher. For information regarding permission, write to Bellwether Media, Inc., Attention: Permissions Department, 6012 Blue Circle Drive, Minnetonka, MN 55343.

Library of Congress Cataloging-in-Publication Data

Names: McDonald, Amy, author.
Title: Deer / by Amy McDonald.
Description: Minneapolis, MN : Bellwether Media, 2021. | Series: Animals in my yard | Includes bibliographical references and index. | Audience: Grades PreK-2
Identifiers: LCCN 2020007064 (print) | LCCN 2020007065 (ebook) | ISBN 9781644873076 (library binding) | ISBN 9781681037943 (paperback) | ISBN 9781681037707 (ebook)
Subjects: LCSH: Deer--Juvenile literature.
Classification: LCC QL737.U55 M359 2021 (print) | LCC QL737.U55 (ebook) | DDC 599.65--dc23
LC record available at https://lccn.loc.gov/2020007064
LC ebook record available at https://lccn.loc.gov/2020007065

Text copyright © 2021 by Bellwether Media, Inc. BLASTOFF! BEGINNERS and associated logos are trademarks and/or registered trademarks of Bellwether Media, Inc.

Editor: Christina Leaf   Designer: Jeffrey Kollock

Printed in the United States of America, North Mankato, MN.

Table of Contents

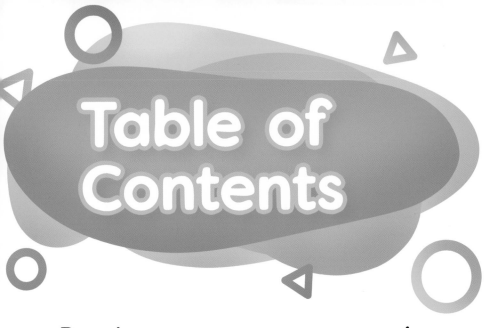

Deer!

Shhh! Look in the grass. Can you see the deer?

Body Parts

Deer have
big ears.
They listen
for danger.

ears

Deer have strong legs and hard **hooves**. They run fast.

hooves

Deer have
brown fur.
It keeps
them warm.

fur

The Lives of Deer

Deer live in forests and fields. They look for food.

Deer eat grass, nuts, and leaves.

grass

nuts

leaves

Wolves and people hunt deer. Deer run from danger.

wolf

This is a **buck**.
He fights with
his **antlers**.

buck

antlers

This is a **doe**.
Can you spot
her baby?

doe

Deer Facts

Deer Body Parts

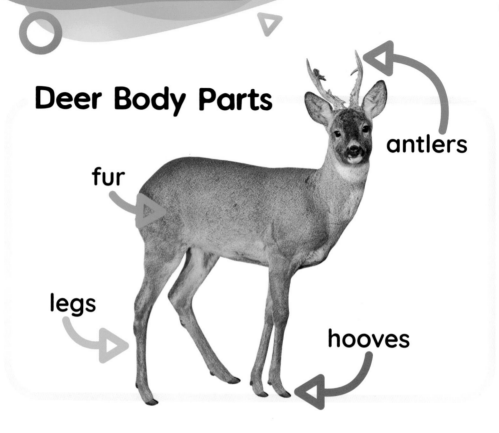

antlers

fur

legs

hooves

Deer Food

grass

nuts

leaves

Glossary

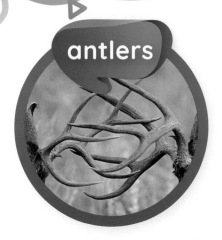

antlers

body parts made of bone that are shed every year

buck

a male deer

doe

a female deer

hooves

the hard tips of animal feet

To Learn More

ON THE WEB

FACTSURFER

Factsurfer.com gives you a safe, fun way to find more information.

1. Go to www.factsurfer.com.

2. Enter "deer" into the search box and click 🔍.

3. Select your book cover to see a list of related content.

Index

The images in this book are reproduced through the courtesy of: sbyun, front cover; Gallinago_media, p. 3; Ondrej Prosicky, pp. 4-5; Inga Locmele, pp. 6-7; Wild Media, pp. 8-9; SWKrullImaging, pp. 10-11; marcin jucha, pp. 12-13; Adriana Margarita Larios Arellano, pp. 14-15; Dark Caramel, p. 14 (grass); Chodimeafotime, p. 15 (nuts); John Swannick, p. 15 (leaves); Darren Baker, p. 16; Mirek Srb, pp. 16-17; Tom Reichner, pp. 18, 23 (antlers); Tony Campbell, pp. 18-19; Geoffrey Kuchera, pp. 20-21; clarst5, p. 22; Bokeh Blur Background, p. 22 (grass); Lubos Chlubny, p. 22 (nuts); Giedriius, p. 22 (leaves); Paul Tessier, p. 23 (buck); David Kalosson, p. 23 (doe); Montri Thipsorn, p. 23 (hooves).